Worksop
Past

Guardian

at heart ♡ publications

First Published in 2007 by:
At Heart Ltd, 32 Stamford Street, Altrincham,
Cheshire, WA14 1EY.

in conjunction with

The Worksop Guardian
21-27 Ryton Street, Worksop, Nottinghamshire,
East Midlands, S80 2AY.

©2007 The Worksop Guardian

All rights reserved. No part of this book may be reproduced in any form or by any means, including information storage and retrieval systems without permission in writing from the publisher, except by a reviewer who may quote passages in a review.

Printed by Bell & Bain, Scotland.

ISBN : 978 1 84547 149 1

Contents

Introduction	4
Around Worksop	5
Entertainment, Leisure, Welfare and Sport	48
By Rail and Road	72
Industry	96
Green and Pleasant Land	112

Introduction

WHEN the *Worksop Guardian* was first published on Friday 27 March 1896, Queen Victoria was still on the throne, cars were an invention for the super-rich, air travel was the stuff of science fiction and the streets and houses were lit by gaslight.

A lot has happened in the past century and, like everywhere else, Worksop has lived through some dramatic changes and events, local, national and worldwide.

Changes in transport, by road, rail and air... changes in industry, with the rise and fall of the coal mines... changes in the local community as previously quiet rural areas have seen a huge growth in housing and population and all the social changes that brings about.

It has all been covered in depth in the *Worksop Guardian* every Friday without fail, through strikes, wars, power cuts and other turbulent times.

Here in this book we have trawled through our archives and called on our readers to send us their photos and memories of a remarkable period of time.

You will find pages of fascinating images capturing a glimpse of a world that was once familiar but has now changed with the times.

Enjoy our marvellous collection of photographs capturing the essence of those bygone days as you embark on a wonderful nostalgic journey through this book.

Our thanks to the many people who provided postcards, slides and photographs from their own private collections who helped make this book possible.

Around Worksop

■ Central Avenue as it was in the 1930s, when the River Ryton burst its banks, a regular occurrence in the town.

Around Worksop

■ The view down Carlton Road from the railway station looking towards Victoria Square. When built during the latter half of the nineteenth century, the dwellings along here housed Worksop's wealthier inhabitants while the Railway Hotel catered for tourists and business people alike. Though listed in Baedeker guides, the Station was described as 'unpretending' with rooms – in 1910 – from 2s 6d a night.

■ The Victorian and Edwardian professional classes loved to clutter up their rooms with furniture and ornaments often from various parts of the Empire. When people at the posh end of Carlton Road were living like this, those experiencing hard times in the poorer parts of the town were sometimes forced to use their doors, windows and floorboards for firewood.

Worksop Past

■ Will Crookes' Drapery and Millinery Stores on Gateford Road.

■ By the 1890s the town was on one of the cross-country Victorian tourist routes due to the close proximity of Welbeck Abbey, Worksop Manor, Clumber Park, Rufford Abbey and Thoresby Hall – all of which opened their grounds to members of the general public, though the Dukes of Portland and Newcastle also opened parts of their houses at Welbeck and Clumber respectively. The picture is of Victoria Square so named to commemorate the Golden Jubilee of Queen Victoria in 1887 though for decades afterwards it was still known by its unofficial name of Common End.

Around Worksop

Worksop Past

■ Families line the street as a marching brass band entertains the crowds.

■ Victoria Square post Second World War with Gateford Road running off to the left and Carlton Road to the right.

Around Worksop

■ Dodgson's shop, Victoria Square.

■ Victoria Square in June 2007 and there is still a post office at the corner with Carlton Road.

Worksop Past

■ Looking from Victoria Square towards the town centre. The large building on the right was the main offices of the Worksop and Retford Brewery Co.

■ The former Worksop and Retford Brewery office block still stands and today is better known as The Litten Tree. (Clive Hardy).

Around Worksop

Worksop Past

Around Worksop

■ Built By James Brindley in the early 1770s the 46-mile long Chesterfield Canal linked Chesterfield with the navigable River Trent at Stockwell Basin where goods were transhipped between canal and river craft. Until the railways or road traffic took over, the canal was heavily used for freight and mineral traffic – Shireoaks Colliery for one shipped coal out via the canal. In Worksop there was an over-canal warehouse – once owned by Pickfords – that allowed goods to be transhipped, while companies such as Smith Brothers' Albion Mill had their own facilities.

Worksop Past

Around Worksop

■ The Empire Day parade is under way with the band in the lead.

■ Worksop's main shopping Street, Bridge Street looking towards the Arcade. Barclays Bank – on the corner of Bridge Street and Newcastle Avenue – was built on land once occupied by the town's cattle market.

Worksop Past

■ Looking in the opposite direction to the previous picture, this view was taken was taken in the mid-1950s.

■ Bridge Street, possibly c1920 when cars were locally taxed according to horse-power. The cheapest annual licence was £2.2.0d for vehicles not exceeding six-and-a-half horse-power, the most expensive was £42 motors over 60hp. There was also an annual licence of fifteen shillings for 'male servants' – any male servant employed to drive a motor car.

Around Worksop

Worksop Past

Around Worksop

■ The Old Ship Inn in Bridge Street is said to be Worksop's oldest pub but when this picture was taken there would have been other claimants to the title including the George Inn which closed in 1909. The George had been one of the most important hostelries in town – a coaching inn and the place where the local magistrates held their monthly meeting. The Old Ship allegedly took its name from timbers used internally during its construction that were salvaged from warships broken up during the Napoleonic Wars. However the building looks far older – probably 16th or 17th century though it is still possible that timber salvaged from ships being broken up were recycled.

■ Bridge Street under water in the floods of 2007.

Worksop Past

■ Forrest's store, Worksop.

Around Worksop

■ This is Bridge Street before the Great War. The Old Ship Inn is to the left of and slightly behind the cameraman.

■ Bridge Street, Worksop.

Worksop Past

Around Worksop

■ North Notts Farm Shop, looking towards Victoria Square.

■ An exterior view of Eyres & Sons Ltd furniture shop, one of the longest established shops in the town, at the top of Bridge Street, still going strong today.

Worksop Past

Looking towards the corner of Watson Road.

■ The Don Jon with Neales in the background.

Around Worksop

■ The town's main post office in Newcastle Avenue was completed in 1909 and officially opened the following year, replacing an earlier one in Potter Street. Had you walked along here in Edwardian times, one of the things you might have noticed was the telegraph poles, each carrying over forty wires radiating out from the post office. A few carried telephone wires but most were for sending and receiving telegram traffic, one of the principal communications systems of the era. In those days it was not unusual for post offices to remain open until 10.00pm.

Worksop Past

Around Worksop

■ A photo of the old Worksop police station on Potter Street taken in the late 1950s.

■ The Greyhound Hotel, Park Street, in the course of demolition. During those long hot Edwardian summers before the outbreak of the Great War, when Worksop was often 'overrun with excursionists from Sheffield and other large towns,' the George was one of the town's main hotels – the others being the Lion, the Royal, and the Station. Edwardian day trippers could enjoy dinner at the George for 2s 6d a head, or pay from 3s a head at either the Lion or the Royal.

Worksop Past

Around Worksop

F.E. Jones' newsagents on Potter Street is either being demolished or it was some party! The street was originally known as Pottergate, taking its name logically from the fact that it was where potters sold their wares from market stalls.

Worksop Past

■ The premises used by Daykins Drug & Herbal store at 9-13 Cheapside was once famous in Worksop as it used to be John Saxton's Abbey Tea Warehouse. As well as a large selection of teas, coffee and cocoa, John stocked an extensive range of provisions and groceries.

■ News of Queen Elizabeth's forthcoming visit to Welbeck Abbey, and the new home for disabled children at Hesley Hall, near Tickhill, in July 1950 had been common knowledge for several months; then on Friday 21st April it was announced that Her Majesty would indeed be paying an official visit to Worksop and the she would be received at the Town Hall by the Mayor and Corporation. The *Worksop Guardian* reported that: 'The date originally fixed for the opening of Hesley Hall was the 25th July, but, whether or not this date is still to be altered, Worksop's great day will, in all probability, be Monday, the 24th of July.

A programme for the Royal visit to Worksop is being worked out with meticulous care by the Town Clerk (Mr. W. A. Williams) and other Council officials, and this will, no doubt, be submitted to Buckingham Palace, after some guidance from the Duke and Duchess of Portland. We understand that Winifred Duchess of Portland will be hostess to Her Majesty and the Royal party at Welbeck Abbey.

It is to be expected that similar arrangements will be made to those which were successfully carried out on the occasion of the visit of H.R.H. the Duchess of Kent in December 1946, when a carpet was laid across the market place to the side entrance of the Town Hall. If the Hesley Hall ceremony is to take place on the same day, it may be presumed that Her Majesty will leave Welbeck after lunch and will drive from the Lion Gates down Sparken Hill to the Town Hall. It may not be possible to allow a longer space of time than a quarter of an hour for the presentation of councillors, officials and their wives, and this would mean that it is unlikely that a formal loyal address will be read.

Business people and other residents of the town are already searching for flags and bunting with which to decorate their premises in order to give a gay and enthusiastic welcome to the Royal visitor.'

Around Worksop

Worksop Past

Around Worksop

■ Walking along the famous red carpet outside the Town Hall. Her visit to Worksop lasted just twenty-two minutes, yet in that time 53 people were presented to her in the Council Chambers. Although children were given a holiday in the sense that school registers would not be marked for the afternoon session, it was anticipated that the majority would still turn up at school after their midday meal whereupon they would be taken to reserved vantage points along the royal route. Later, Her Majesty inspected a royal guard of honour drawn up from troops of the Royal Electrical and Mechanical Engineers.

■ Queen Elizabeth receives an enthusiastic welcome from the people of Worksop. Earlier in the year the Rev P. J. Powlesland had written to the palace seeking the donation of an item that could be sold off at a forthcoming Spring Fayre that was to be held to raise funds for the former Salvation Army Hall that the St Luke's Church had recently acquired. The response was a 26-piece canteen of cutlery complete with a letter from the Queen, through her Lady-in-Waiting, wishing the Rev Powlesland success in his aims. Around £1,500 was still needed to complete the purchase and renovate the place which would be used for social activities, youth work and Sunday school.

Worksop Past

Around Worksop

■ Twenty-seven years on from the previous picture and Worksop town is trimmed up ready for another royal visit only this time it is the Silver Jubilee visit of Queen Elizabeth II in 1977. In the background, Eyres furniture shop on Bridge Street can be seen and to the left of the picture would be the local market. Let's hope the litter was tidied up.

■ People gather outside Eyres & Sons Ltd to greet the Queen Elizabeth. On the right of the picture is a sign, which reads 'Worksop Welcomes Her Majesty The Queen with Loyal Greetings.'

Worksop Past

Around Worksop

■ From the top of Bridge Street looking down the crowd awaits the arrival of Queen Elizabeth II during her Silver Jubilee tour of the country.

■ Staff at the Central School in 1953. Amongst those pictured are Mr Cole, Mr Bailey, Mr Mather and Mr Solway.

Worksop Past

■ Staff and pupils at Central School in 1955. Pictured are: Ronald Dixon, Leslie Fisher, Brian Ward, Brian Hewitt, Richard Salmon, John Smith, Robin Linacre, John Titmuss, Ian Bell, Jimmy McLeon, Louis Smith, Mr Thornton, Diana Thompson, Sandra, Pauline, Jeanie and Maureen.

■ Children enjoying fun and games at playtime at Newcastle Street School in 1963.

Around Worksop

■ Two well-known figures around Worksop – Ned and Flo. Ned was born into a wealthy family but fell in love with Flo, one of the maids. Upon his marriage to Flo, he was thrown out of the family home and left to fend for himself. Together, Ned and Flo would wander around the streets of Worksop with all their worldly possessions in a battered old pram.

■ Dating from 1803 and built twenty or so years after a visit to the town by John Wesley, the Methodist church was seriously damaged by fire in June 1969 and had to be completely rebuilt.

Worksop Past

■ This picture of the priory gatehouse predates the £550 restoration of 1912. The porch to the right of the gateway was built by John Talbot, First Earl of Shrewsbury in memory of his wife Maude de Furnival. It leads to a pilgrims' shrine.

Around Worksop

■ Echoes of Worksop's feudal past. Maude de Furnival had already lost her husband, Sir Gerald de Furnival, lord of the manor of Worksop, who, according to some published sources had died in Jerusalem in 1219 whilst taking part in the Third Crusade. However the Third Crusade had come to an abrupt end in 1187 with the destruction of the Christian army by Saladin at the battle of Hattin. Not only that but the Holy City was forced to surrender and had been in Arab hands ever since. There was a crusade taking place in 1219 but that was against Damietta and led by the Holy Roman Emperor Frederick II. He as an unusual man for a western ruler at that time in that not only was he a skilled linguist – he spoke six languages including Arabic, but he had also read the Holy Koran. It is not impossible for Sir Gerald to have been in Jerusalem in 1219 as Saladin had declared the city open to all Muslims, Jews and Christians who wished to visit for religious reasons. Hot on the news of Sir Gerald's death came word that Maude's eldest son Thomas had also died. In her grief Maude ordered her younger son, Gerald to the Holy Land: his quest being to locate the body of his brother, recover the heart, and bring it safely back so that it could be interred in the priory.

Worksop Past

■ Taken around the late 1970s or early 1980s, this photo is of the Worksop shopping precinct, which is now the Priory Centre.

■ The site selected for town's memorial to those killed during the Great War was on an island in the middle of a new road linking Watson Road and the Priory Church of St Mary and St Cuthbert.

■ Netherholme Shopping Precinct with the old Tesco store to the right of the picture and the town's nightclub in the background.

Around Worksop

Worksop Past

■ People stand amazed, looking at the flood waters on Newcastle Avenue, while others try to make their way along the street in the summer floods of 2007.

■ Worksop floods of the past show how streets, homes and businesses were affected by the rising waters.

Around Worksop

Entertainment, Leisure, Welfare and Sport

■ The residents of Carlton Close elected to hold their VJ Day celebrations in the Worksop and Retford Brewery's cricket pavilion. The pavilion is no more: it was demolished to make way for housing.

Entertainment, Leisure, Welfare and Sport

■ At 2.41am on Monday, 7 May 1945 Germany surrendered unconditionally. Hostilities were to end at one minute past midnight of Tuesday, which was then declared by the government Victory in Europe (VE) Day and a public holiday extending into Wednesday 9 May. VE Day saw streets everywhere burst miraculously into colour with flags and bunting, setting the scene for street parties for children as well as impromptu singing and dancing. Residents joined together, pooling their rations to come up with spreads of cakes, sandwiches, custard, jelly and blancmange, and, considering the scarcity of materials, some streets even managed to get their kids into fancy dress. The defeat of Japan in August 1945 brought with it another two days of celebrations and street parties. Our picture shows the celebrations in Aldred Street. People stand amazed, looking at the flood waters on Newcastle Avenue, while others try to make their way along the street in the summer floods of 2007.

■ Children's Christmas Party 1950s style.

Worksop Past

Entertainment, Leisure, Welfare and Sport

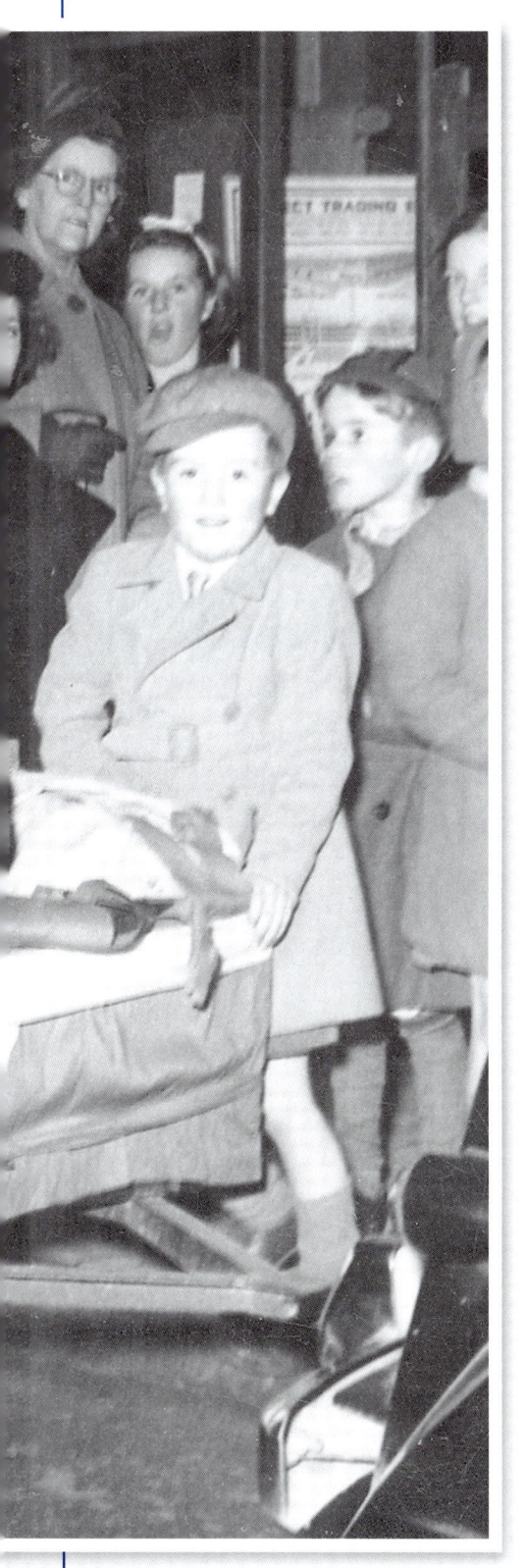

■ *A Midsummer Night's Dream* staged at St Anne's Hall was a joint effort by several drama groups to commemorate the Coronation of Queen Elizabeth II.

■ It is around 1950 and rationing is still in force even though the war had ended in 1945. The best Santa can hope for on his visit to Worksop in 'export or die' Britain is a tow along Eastgate behind a saloon car.

Worksop Past

Entertainment, Leisure, Welfare and Sport

■ 'Busman's Ball' taken in the 1950s at the Palais De Dance on Newcastle Avenue.

■ A 'Busmans Holiday' during the early 1960s on a day's outing to Blackpool. Pictured are the drivers and conductors of East Midland Motor Services. Back Row: John Harrison, Bill Cadman, John Allen, Bill Bows, unknown, Maurice Bradley, Ted Lewis and Jim Forman. Front Row: Pat Allen (Joinson), unknown, Pat Ringer, Beryl Reaney (Bows), unknown, unknown, Ann Harrison, Stephanie Forman (Potts), Madge Chambers (Forman).

■ In 1954, the local drama festival put on a play called *The Dear Departed*. Back Row L-R: Irene Hardy, Peter Hall, Brian Sims, Robin Linacre, Pat Roper. Front Row L-R: Jean Pressley, Diana Thompson, Wendy Thorpe.

Worksop Past

■ Worksop Town Brass Band in 1860.

■ Worksop Town Band.

Entertainment, Leisure, Welfare and Sport

■ Lambs Elite Band.

Worksop Past

■ 'Duck' (Dorsay) Pearson and Ed (Lang) Brooks better known as the 'Backyard Buskers.'

Entertainment, Leisure, Welfare and Sport

■ Creswell Colliery Welfare Bugle Band during September 1953.

■ Mary, the owner of the Lion Vaults pictured with Mel Atkins.

Worksop Past

■ The circus pays its annual visit to Worksop. Elephants are led through Priorswell Road car park in 1968.

■ Members of the Lion Vaults Fishing Club include: Ron Chamberlin, Lou Pingree, Fudge Bone, Mel Atkins, Les Lee, Jock Macloud, Vic Sibson, Kiff Morris (Landlord), John Stringfellow, Terry Pywell, Harry Emson, Did Neal, Ron, Ray Kirton.

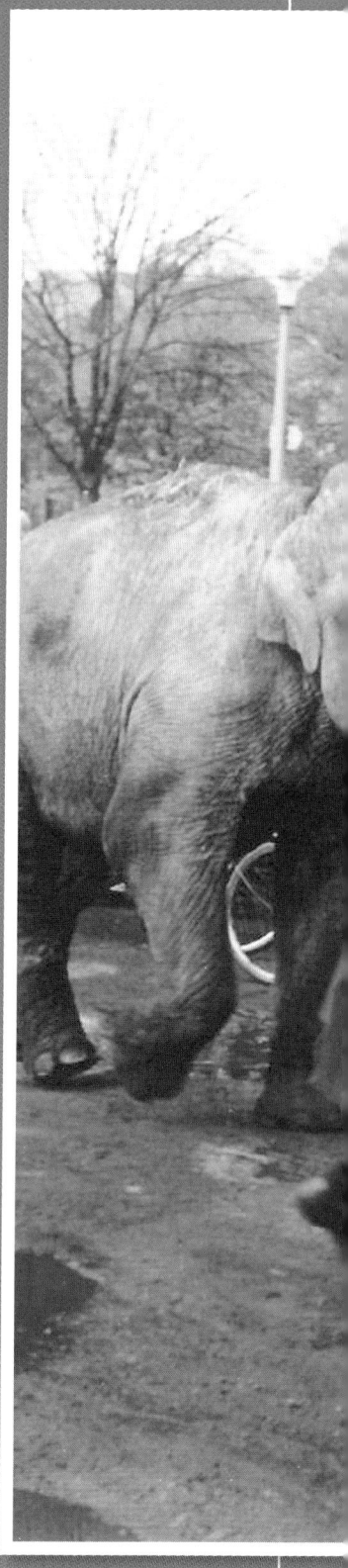

Entertainment, Leisure, Welfare and Sport

Worksop Past

■ The Victoria Hospital was the result of the people of Worksop's intention to celebrate the 1897 Diamond Jubilee of Queen Victoria with something a little more permanent than a civic reception and a procession. Paid for by public subscription the five-bed cottage hospital on Watson Road opened on 24 May 1900. This tiny hospital represented a major shift in medical care in the town as locals had previously had to travel miles (Sheffield or Nottingham) to undergo anything other than the most basic of surgical procedures.

■ A couple of years prior to the outbreak of the Great War the Victoria Hospital underwent a major extension programme with the addition of the Coronation wing and a Children's ward. Further extensions followed during the 1920s.

Entertainment, Leisure, Welfare and Sport

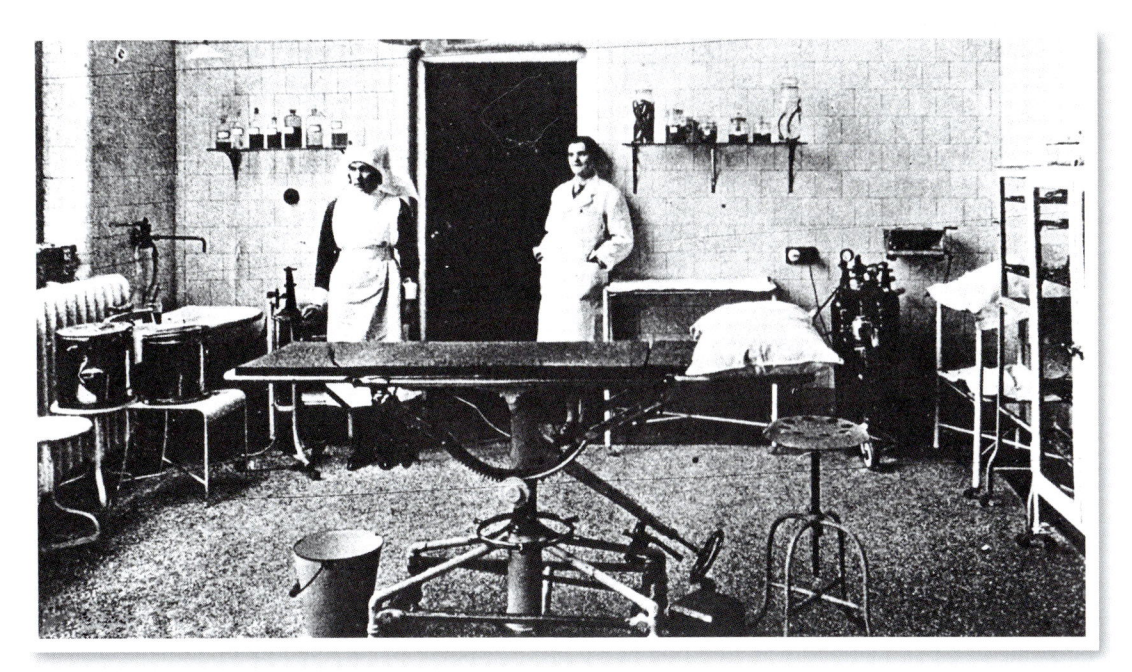

■ The operating theatre at Victoria Hospital.

■ The Men's Ward at Victoria Hospital in the days when during doctors' rounds the freshly scrubbed patient had to lie rigidly to attention – arms outside the blankets pressed firmly to the side of the body, legs together, and under no circumstances whatsoever was doctor to be engaged in conversation. Sometimes a post-op patient might sit by the side of his bed, hair combed, arms folded, head held back – neither slouching nor talking tolerated.

Worksop Past

Entertainment, Leisure, Welfare and Sport

■ British troops recovering from their wounds pose with members of the Kilton nursing staff in this postcard dating from the Great War.

■ This postcard of Kilton Hill Infirmary was probably taken prior to the outbreak of the Great War because during which the lawns and gardens were dug up so that vegetables could be grown.

Worksop Past

■ Bassetlaw District General is now the only hospital serving the town.

■ How the NHS used to be in Worksop – a photo of the old Victoria Hospital, just off Memorial Avenue, taken around the 1970s. Today, the building has been replaced with a supermarket and various shops.

Entertainment, Leisure, Welfare and Sport

Worksop Past

Entertainment, Leisure, Welfare and Sport

■ Creswell Nursing Cadets taken 14 May 1961.

■ Red Cross Day at Welbeck – it is thought the lady is the Duchess of Portland, taken during the early days of the Great War and was one of many events hosted by the estate. On 10 August 1914 a meeting was held in Worksop Town Hall for 'Women Helpers' to come forward and do their bit for king and country. Over three hundred ladies volunteered to make clothes – usually socks, scarves, gloves etc, for distribution to troops, sailors, refugees – whilst nearly another hundred put their names down to form an ambulance unit.

Worksop Past

■ The first recipient of the meals on wheels in Worksop was Mrs Eliza Mottisha.

■ The Worksop Cricket Club Saturday first XI as it was in 1914, the year the team triumphed in the Bassetlaw League.

Entertainment, Leisure, Welfare and Sport

■ Manton Colliery Athletic Club, the Bassetlaw Cricket League champions and *Worksop Guardian* Cup winners. Pictured Top Row – G. Godley (chairman), S. Martin (committee), A. Walker (committee), G. Raynes (vice chairman), B. H. Pickering (manager at colliery), T. Seddon (committee), E. Stone (committee), and E. Topham (league secretary).
2nd Row – F. Charlesworth (committee), T. Spencer, W. Smith, J. Malthouse, Jim Stocks, B. Jones, S. Godley, J. Winrow, G. Limb (treasurer). Bottom Row – T. Harrison (secretary), H. Davis, E. Alletson (vice chairman), Joe Stocks (captain), B. Floyd, G. Wass, A. Ridley (scorer).

Worksop Past

■ Those were the days! The Canch open air swimming pool was a popular place in the 1930s.

Entertainment, Leisure, Welfare and Sport

By Road and Rail

■ Horse drawn landau carriage.

By Road and Rail

■ The Smith Brothers' fleet of steam lorries line up for the cameraman at Albion Mills. Smiths also used horses, and on 5 September 1908 six of them were used to haul a fully operational sea-going lifeboat through the town to Beards Dam, where it was launched and put through its paces in front of an audience of 4000 people. The boat, from Tramore in County Waterford, was the highlight of Worksop's first ever lifeboat day.

■ The Worksop Brewery fleet.

Worksop Past

By Road and Rail

■ Eyres delivery vans through the ages – well from the 1920s to the advent of the Bedford Dormobile.

■ An old picture of the Lion Gates, leading to the Welbeck Estate. Although the date of the photo is not known, judging by the type of cars, it is probably around the 1930s.

Worksop Past

■ Water, water everywhere: another casualty of the late 1950s flood was the East Midland garage, Worksop. Amongst those pictured are: George Morris, 'Dusty' Rhodes, Jolly Tarr, Reg Simons and Roy Mangham. The bus is one of a batch of AEC Regal IIIs fitted with Weymann 35-seat bodies that were delivered to East Midland during 1949 and which are easily identified from earlier single-deckers because of their large destination screen box.

By Road and Rail

■ On the outbreak of the Second World War the Government imposed a complete stoppage on the construction of new buses, both to save on materials and because there was vital war work to be assigned to manufacturers. To make matters worse, many buses were requisitioned by the armed forces or for ARP work. Bryan Barton of Barton Buses was still at school in September 1939 and earned his pocket money cleaning buses at the weekend at their Long Eaton depot. He remembered that just two days prior to the declaration of war no less than forty-four of their drivers who were military reservists were called up. That wasn't all, and before the month was out, twenty-one of Barton's brand new 39-seat saloons had been requisitioned by the armed forces and taken to Chilwell where they were given a coat of drab grey paint.

By the end of 1939 many operators including East Midland were struggling to maintain services: the answer was a standard Austerity-pattern bus, the specification of which included a reduction in the amount of metal used in the bodywork, a limited number of opening windows, destination indicators on the front only, and slatted wooden seats. As supplies of these vehicles would be limited the Ministry of War Transport assumed responsibility for their allocation and though operators could state their preference for a particular type of vehicle they had to take pot luck on what actually turned up. Between 1942 and 1945 East Midland Motor Services were allocated a total of eleven lowbridge type Guy Arabs and a Bristol K5G, which meant that many of their pre-war buses survived longer in service than they would otherwise have done, and when East Midland took over Baker Brothers, of Warsop, in 1945, several more Guy Arabs were added to the fleet. This photo of a Guy Arab was taken at Abbey Cross bus stop on the number 4 route from Manton's Hardwick Road East service through the town centre to Coggan Street now known as Gateford Avenue. The fare was 4d.

Worksop Past

■ During 1947-48 East Midland Motor Services took delivery of fourteen AEC Regal IIIs chassis all of which were given Leyland bodies dating from before the Second World War. In 1952 they were refitted with new Willowbrook bodies of the type shown here on K12.

By Road and Rail

■ In 1958 East Midland took over the fleet of Wass Brothers Ltd of Mansfield, which included three Cravens-bodied ex-London Transport RT double-deckers. However they didn't survive all that long as the company had already placed orders for new Leyland Atlantean front-loading, rear-engined double-deckers. All three RTs were withdrawn during 1960.

By the early 1950s the Austerity-pattern Guy Arab double-deckers were getting past their sell-by dates, and though a number of Leyland Titan PD1 and PD2/1s had joined the East Midland fleet, supplies of new buses were still relatively scarce. This was due partly to the Government requiring British industry to concentrate on overseas, so that we could get our hands on much-needed foreign exchange, and also because just about every operator in the country was screaming for new buses. Along with many others, East Midland resorted to stop gap measures, and during 1953-54 sent a number of Arabs to be rebodied. This rebodied Guy Arab photographed outside Wakefield's Army Stores on Bridge Place was picking up passengers en-route from Gateford Road to Manton. This was in the days when there was two-way traffic through Worksop town centre.

Worksop Past

By Road and Rail

■ The North Ring Road looking towards Gateford. This picture was taken on the same day as the previous one.

■ This almost traffic free view of the North Ring Road at Worksop was taken in January 1967. Between 1960 and 1970 annual sales of new cars rose from between 820,000 to 1,127,000 but they were still out of the range of most people, for as well as paying for the car, the customer also had to pay the Government purchase tax at around 36 per cent. The first Japanese imports had arrived in 1965, but the numbers were small and considered to be of no consequence by British motor manufacturers.

Worksop Past

■ In November 1984 work began on the construction of Worksop's A57 by-pass, the completion of which would allow some through traffic to skirt the town and ease congestion on the ring road and within the town centre.

■ Work in progress on the A57 Worksop by-pass in May 1985 with the excavation of the cutting near Manton well under way.

By Road and Rail

■ The A57 Worksop by-pass had to be elevated near Rhodesia so that it would clear Tylden Road, the Chesterfield Canal and Shireoaks Road.

■ Michael Spicer, Under Secretary of State for Transport cuts the tape to officially open the Worksop by-pass on 1 May 1986. Holding the tape, from left, are Coun Alan Shaw, vice chairman of Notts County Council, and Coun Dennis Wells, chairman of Bassetlaw Council.

Worksop Past

■ When this picture of road widening in progress on the Chesterfield – Worksop Road at Red Hill, Whitwell in June 1960 was taken, a steam-powered road-roller was amongst the items of hardware being used. Our picture looks across to the Half Moon Inn and Worksop.

■ Creswell village was once served by two stations: one on the Great Central line, the other on the Midland line to Mansfield. To avoid confusion the Great Central station was renamed Creswell & Welbeck in September 1897, while the Midland station was appearing in the timetables as Elmton & Creswell from May 1886. Creswell & Welbeck closed to passengers on 10 September 1939 – a victim of wartime rationalisation – and closed completely on 28 November 1949. Elmton & Creswell closed to goods traffic on 6 January 1964 and to passengers during the following October, though private sidings remained in use a little while longer.

By Road and Rail

■ Whitwell station on the Midland Railway line from Mansfield Woodhouse to Worksop. The line closed to passenger services on 12 October 1964 but remained open for goods traffic until 14 June the following year when it closed completely.

■ After Whitwell closed, the station building was dismantled stone-by-stone and taken to the Midland Railway Centre at Butterley, Derbyshire where was re-erected. (Clive Hardy)

Worksop Past

By Road and Rail

■ Built for the LNER in 1923 and sold out of service by BR in 1963, the *Flying Scotsman* was the first privately owned steam locomotive allowed to work on the UK main line. She is seen here belting through Worksop in 1968, the year British Railways withdrew the last of its steam locomotives save for three engines that worked the narrow gauge Vale of Rheidol line in Wales. In 1929 *Flying Scotsman* starred in the first British-made feature film with sound, and on 30th November 1934 she became the first steam locomotive in the UK to officially reach 100mph whilst hauling a special test train between Kings Cross and Leeds. From August 1968 she was the only steam locomotive in the country that was allowed to run on BR.

■ Within a few years of services being withdrawn between Mansfield Woodhouse and Worksop via Whitwell, Creswell and Shirebrook etc, it became apparent that the overall increase in population in the area, as well as the fact that more and more people were commuting to work, there were grounds for reopening the line to passenger traffic. As Worksop's station had been dismantled and moved to Butterley, the village got a new one when the Robin Hood Line reopened for passenger traffic. (Clive Hardy)

Worksop Past

■ Designed for the Manchester, Sheffield and Lincolnshire Railway by architects Weightmann & Hadfield and opened in July 1849, Worksop station was quite an ornate affair. Given the town's close proximity to the Dukeries the MS&LR would want to make a good impression on the ladies and gentlemen of the leisured classes so much so that nearly £8,000 was spent on its construction out of white Steetley stone.

■ The 1040hrs Central Trains service for Nottingham via Whitwell, Creswell, Langwith Whaley Thorns, Shirebrook, Mansfield Woodhouse, Mansfield, Sutton Parkway, Kikby-in-Ashfield, Hucknall and Bulwell, waits to depart from Worksop on Wednesday 11 July 2007. (Clive Hardy)

By Road and Rail

Worksop Past

By Road and Rail

■ Worksop station looks today (2007) much like it did in the 1850s. Its architects Weightmann & Hadfield were also responsible designing Sheffield Victoria station (opened 1851) and the massive 660yd forty-arch railway viaduct in Sheffield, better known as the Wicker Arches. Their work outside the railway included the Cathedral Church of St Marie, Norfolk Row, Sheffield, which in 1980 became the seat of the Bishop of Hallam. (Clive Hardy)

■ The merry-go-round (mgr) train concept was introduced during 1965 to provide the CEGB's new generation of coal-fired power stations with a constant supply of coal. A number of collieries were re-equipped with rapid loading systems – the first was at Langwith Colliery – enabling trains of thirty or more coal wagons to be loaded in less than one hour. On arrival at the mgr equipped power station, the train would take a circular route at slow speed through the complex, each wagon being unloaded automatically as the train passed over the power station's coal hopper conveyor. To operate the service, BR invested in a fleet of new high-capacity coal wagons, and had the gears on a number of diesel locomotives modified enabling them to haul mgr trains at ultra low speed (0.5mph) when loading or discharging. By the late 1990s Worksop was the principal staging post for mgr trains bound for West Burton, Cottam and High Marnham power stations with coal supplied by Gascoigne Wood, Rossington, Harworth, Clipstone, Welbeck, Oxcroft, Thoresby, Rufford and Bilsthorpe collieries/loading points.

Worksop Past

By Road and Rail

■ A trio of HAA coal wagons in trouble at Shireoaks in September 1982. By this time there were more than 10,000 of these wagons in service.

■ A small crowd of onlookers watch BR's recovery operation of a rake of derailed HAA coal wagons at Worksop in 1970.

Worksop Past

By Road and Rail

■ In December 1982 BR unveiled the first of its new 3300hp Class 58 diesel-electric freight locomotives which were capable of hauling mgr trains single-handedly, whereas some of the earlier diesels had to work either in multiple throughout or be given assistance for part of their journey – such as the Class 47 hauled mgr trains from Worksop, which were assisted by another locomotive as far as Dinnington.

■ The Chairman of the Bassetlaw Council, Coun David, named Class 58 diesel-electric 58034 *Bassetlaw* at a ceremony at Worksop station on 12th December 1985. Also pictured are Mrs Ivy Wells, Eric Straw, Area Manager British Rail and Colin Driver the Director of Freight British Rail.

■ English Welsh & Scottish Railways (EWS) Canadian-built 3300hp locomotive 66009 eases through Worksop at the head of a rake of EWS 102tonne bogie coal hoppers on Wednesday 11th July 2007. (Clive Hardy)

Industry

■ Frank Coney, Dukeries Mill.

Industry

■ Smith Brothers' Albion Mill was completed in 1906. This picture was taken in 2007 and shows the original building together with modern extensions to the business. (Clive Hardy)

■ Associated British Maltsters Ltd. It is hard to imagine in 2007 just how important the malting industry had been in the economic development of Worksop, because by the time Victoria came to the throne there were over twenty active maltings in the area. Though these were relatively small-scale outfits, the coming of the railways opened up opportunities for larger operations, the first being the Clinton Maltings, owned by brewer John Threlfall of Manchester, which was in full production by 1852.

Worksop Past

■ The old Worksop Brewery. In 1881 the Priorswell Brewery Co and Smith and Nephew amalgamated to form the Worksop and Retford Brewery Company. As part of the new company's rationalisation process, brewing was henceforth concentrated at the Priorswell Road site, which was expanded to increase its overall capacity.

■ The Old Worksop Brewery.

Industry

■ Originally sunk by the Wigan Coal Corporation between 1898 and 1904, Manton Colliery produced its first coal in 1907. On nationalisation in 1947, Manton was assigned to the NCB's North Eastern Division, Area No1 along with Firbeck, Shireoaks and Steetley collieries. Our picture dates from 1967 following a major reorganisation by the NCB. The Divisions were replaced by Areas - Manton, Shireoaks and Steetley were transferred to the newly created South Yorkshire Area of twenty pits which included the likes of Manvers Main, Orgreave, Cortonwood, Wath Main and Elsecar Main.

Worksop Past

■ Workers outside Shireoaks Colliery drift in 1978. The Shireoaks Colliery Co was registered in December 1864, though the colliery itself dated back to the previous decade – the shaft having been sunk from March 1854 and the first coal being reached in February 1859. The company had mining interests throughout the area and in May 1873 work began on sinking the shaft at a new colliery at Steetley. Both Shireoaks and Steetley were allocated to the NCB's North East Division, No1 Area on nationalisation in 1947. In March 1967 both collieries were transferred to the South Yorkshire Area and in March 1983 these two collieries were merged thereby bringing surface working at Steetley to an end. In April 1990 the merged colliery was transferred to the South Yorkshire Group and closed a month later.

■ Whitwell Colliery was sunk by the Shireoaks Colliery Co during 1890-91 and was deepened during the 1920s.

Industry

■ Sunk by the Bolsover Colliery Co during the mid-1890s and completed in the early 1900s Creswell Colliery once held the world record for winding coal when 3800 tons were brought to the surface in a single day.

■ Creswell Colliery c1926.

Worksop Past

Industry

■ Tuesday 26th September 1950 is a day that will be long remembered in Creswell. The day when it became that village's turn to share in the cost of coal as the banner headlines of the *Worksop Guardian* stated: "CRESWELL'S SORROW SHARED. Country-wide expressions of sympathy – Mine Disaster Puts Our Area In Mourning". The newspaper's report read as follows:

"IT is our sorrowful duty this week to have to record the most serious mining disaster for many years. This occurred at Creswell Colliery on Tuesday when, following a fire underground 80 men were overcome by smoke and fumes. They were caught behind a barrier of flame, their escape impossible, and within a few hours came the official announcement that all hope had to be abandoned. Rescue efforts, carried on with total regard of personal safety so characteristic of the miner, were of no further avail. It was realised before 12 noon that none of the men could be alive and further rescue attempts would inevitably lead to loss of life among the specially trained rescue teams who had rushed to the mine. From the time an underground worker reported the fire by phone to the surface, to the posting of a notice at the pit head stating that rescue workers were rapidly on the job, but in spite of their efforts it was not possible to rescue any of the trapped men, only eight hours had elapsed.

Our pictures show relatives, friends and workmates of the trapped men anxiously awaiting news. After the statement announcing that there was no hope for the men cut off by the fire, the Vicar of Creswell, the Rev. C.S.Branson, led the crowd in prayer."

Worksop Past

■ Volunteers including schoolboys, miners and soldiers fill sandbags at the pithead. The bags were then taken underground and used to seal off the fire. It would be over a year before the bodies could be recovered.

■ Sir Hubert Houldsworth, chairman of the NCB East Midlands Division; MP Philip Noel Baker, Minister of Fuel and Power; and Lord Hyndley, chairman of the NCB, get an up to the minute situation report from rescuers who had just returned to the surface.

Industry

■ The villagers of Creswell turn out to pay their respects as one of the victims of the pit disaster is brought to the cemetery.

■ Taken a few days before its official unveiling in April 1952, this is the memorial window installed in Creswell parish church in memory of the miners who died in the Creswell Colliery disaster. Paid for by public subscription, the window was unveiled by Sir Hubert Houldsworth, chairman of the NCB East Midlands Division, and dedicated by the Assistant Bishop of Derby. The inscription reads "Dedicated to the Glory of God and those who have given their lives to the mining industry, and in memory of the 80 men who perished in the Creswell Colliery Disaster 26th September, 1950."

A direct result of the Creswell disaster – which had been caused by the frictional heating of a damaged rubber conveyor-belt – was the replacement of all such belts in every mine in the country with belts made from non-flammable PVC. The disaster was also a factor in the banning of miners under the age of sixteen from working underground and in the later development of the 'Self-Rescuer' breathing mask; easily deployed in an emergency the mask converted carbon monoxide – the main killer in underground fires – into harmless carbon dioxide.

Worksop Past

■ Tom Hendley, Face Chargeman, Creswell Colliery.

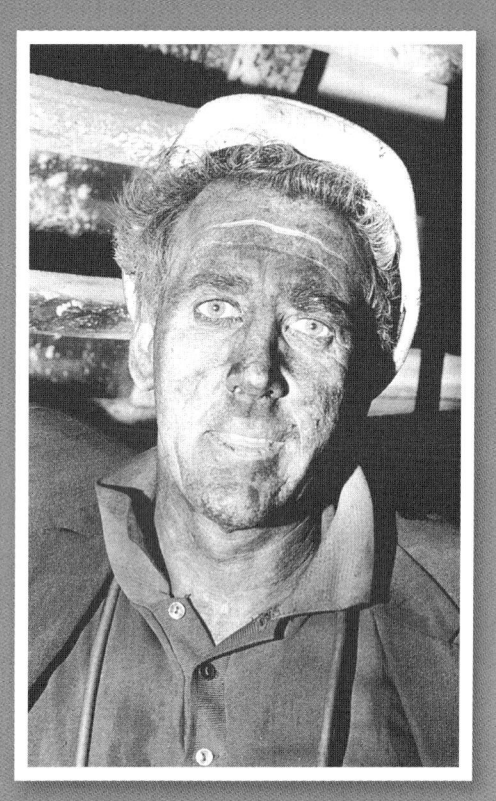

■ Cable-hauled manrider trains were used at Creswell Colliery – the continuous cable can clearly be seen in this picture. As can be seen on picture of Shireoaks colliery, cable haulage was employed there too though it was in conjunction with traditional railway track.

Industry

■ This is Coronation Street, Dinnington, in April 1975.

Worksop Past

■ Dinnington Colliery dates back to 1899 and an original project by the Sheffield Coal Co, but the costs of sinking a deep pit from scratch was such that the company was forced to look for a partner which they found in the Sheepbridge Coal & Iron Co. Sinking finally commenced during 1902, coal being struck in August 1904.

Industry

■ Dawn on 12th November 1984 during the year-long Miners' Strike and after a night which had seen a fair amount of violence around Dinnington Colliery a burnt out car lies on its back.

Worksop Past

Industry

■ Despite the best efforts of these school children the politically driven wholesale destruction of Britain's coal mining industry would continue unabated.

■ Sunk between 1923 and 1925 Firbeck Main Colliery was a joint venture between the Sheepbridge Company and the Doncaster Collieries Association and on nationalisation in 1947, it was placed in the NCB North Eastern Division, Area No1. In March 1967 Firbeck was assigned to the South Yorkshire Area along with Shireoaks, Steetley and Manton. Firbeck closed in November 1968.

Green and Pleasant Land

■ The Blue Bell.

Green and Pleasant Land

■ Traditionally the maypole was set up in the village green and was made from either hawthorn or birch. The pole would be decorated with multicolour ribbons with which dancers would weave in intricate patterns so the ribbons twisted down the maypole until the dancers met at the base of the pole.

■ A 1920s horse drawn parade through the streets of Worksop.

Worksop Past

■ The old cattle market was situated at the junction of Bridge Place and Newcastle Avenue. It was around here on the second Wednesday in November that the annual hiring fair for farm labourers and servants was held as that was the day on which previous annual agreements expired. Hirer and prospective employee haggled terms which were taken as binding when the farmer handed over an advance of one shilling. By the late 1880s farm hands could expect to earn between £12 and £23 a year depending on their skills while boys were paid between £5 and £8. Females, who were often employed as servants, could earn between £9 and £13 a year while girls were paid between £3.10s and £6. In 1900 the market was moved to a new site on what would become known as Memorial Avenue.

■ Livestock Market - The local Livestock Market with a view of Priory Church in the background.

Green and Pleasant Land

Worksop Past

■ Milk delivered straight from the churn was once a daily sight in towns and villages the length and breadth of the country. Worksop was no exception and in the late 1920s Mary Devraux (aged 17) did the rounds on behalf of the local Co-op.

■ Feeding time at Clumber Park in 1965.

Green and Pleasant Land

■ The Canch Mill once belonged to the Priory, though by the Edwardian era the buildings were being used for timber storage and a chairmaking workshop by W. Bramer & Sons until destroyed by fire in 1912.

■ The twin towers of the Priory Church of St Mary and St Cuthbert hold centre stage in this picture of The Canch. The priory was founded in 1103 by William de Lovetot, lord of the manor of Worksop and dedicated to that God-fearing misogynist St Cuthbert: St Mary was a later addition. The twenty or so Augustine monks who lived and prayed here also grew liquorice as a crop, the cultivation of which lasted locally for several centuries after the monastery had been dissolved.

Worksop Past

Green and Pleasant Land

■ This image of the Canch was taken in December 1967 when plans were announced to fill in part of it - approximately the area to the left of the swan in the middle of the picture - so that the park could be extended.

■ The Harrison family hard at work on their farm at Belph in 1922-23. One major annual boost to the local economy of Worksop was the pea harvest. For a couple of weeks or so every July the locals – especially women and children – could earn anything up to five shillings a day picking peas. The whole operation was organised with an almost military precision, thereby enabling peas picked in the morning to be on sale by the same afternoon or evening in London, Birmingham, Derby, Nottingham, Manchester, Sheffield and several other large towns and cities. The bulk of the crop was sent out by rail.

Worksop Past

■ Drilling wheat in October 1939 on grassland which had been ploughed up under the Government's "Grow More Food" campaign to increase production of essential crops. On the outbreak of war the Government effectively took control of British farming through its network of War Agricultural Committees. In an attempt to place as much land as possible under cultivation, the Government offered farmers financial assistance. However, farmers refusing to comply with the demands made by their local War Agricultural Committees or failing to achieve targets set by the ministry were liable to eviction without compensation.

■ Taken some time during the Second World War, these tractors are held in store awaiting distribution to farms around the north-east Derbyshire, north-west Notts area. The Government's commitment to maximising the amount of land under cultivation brought with it a rapid increase in farm mechanisation. At the outbreak of the war it is estimated that there were about 45,000 tractors in use within the UK farming industry – by its end and despite fuel rationing, there were over 200,000 tractors in use as well as a large range of machinery.